Navigate

Navigate

poems by

Karin Schimke

Publication © Modjaji Books 2017
Text © Karin Schimke 2017
First published in 2017 by Modjaji Books
modjajibooks.co.za
ISBN print: 978-1-928215-26-4
e-book: 978-1-928215-56-1
Book and cover design: Megan Ross
Cover artwork: Tammy Griffin
Author photograph: Paul Reeves

Set in Crimson Text 11 pt

Contents

my lips blister, my tongue dries.
atonal winds, weather all wall-eyed.

Myopia

My father had a monocle
for the myriad mysteries
he could fix and unpick.
Sometimes I would lie
on the couch with my foot
in his lap by the light
and watch him clench the
monocle with his brow,
pursing the muscles
round his eye, pursing
his lips for a tuneless
whistle while he pricked
and tweezed at a splinter
in my toe. However
long it took, however sore
it was, losing the splinter
was always a loss.

The workshop

The day had whined and hammered too long.
Plank alignments lay beneath my hands,
a frown like a cocked gun across your forehead.
We sweated. You measured. You planned.
When I shifted my weight, you cursed.
Boredom grew. I needed to pee.
My hands uncramped themselves.
My mouth excused me.
You shouted. My fingers swore.
Relief is enough breath for one last stand.

You grabbed me by the hair.

The immigrant

When the stars are upturned,
north is further away than it's ever been.
The immigrant dims his eyes until there's
just enough dark to see.

Where is his gravity?

The immigrant belongs to nothing
but his hands. There is nothing
to believe in but the joining
of materials, in wood glue and screws,
in the fungus of melted metal
that grows on the joints of steel rods,
or the scrape and shift of wet cement
mixed to fix the cracks in the driveway.

To splice. To knit. To couple. To tie.
These are a kind of gravity.

            You avoid mirrors when the centre is dark
            and the moon is irreparable. When you must shave,
            you lean in so close your breath clouds your image.

He thinks:

Awl
Trowel
Spade
Barrow
Gloves

See? I know the words
for navigation and survival
in this ugly language.

When the cloud fades to expose
your reflected cheek, stubbling
a white brush against the loose land
of your face, you remember perhaps
a small mirror in a dark kitchen up north
– blacker hair, paler skin.
You still have that passport.

He doesn't belong here.
He doesn't belong there.
There is no ampersand.
He belongs to his hands.

Belonging is as delicate as a machine:
one foreign speck of dust makes each part
question itself. You must keep the system clean.

Every time something breaks
the immigrant curses a drawer-full
of clattering consonants. He takes
the thing apart. Rummages for
for cogs for screws for washers
for clamps hammers files
until it ticks or hums again.
But always a little off then,
always a little less than before.
He tinkers to keep damaged things going.

Your hands give you your best gravity.
And you dim the eye. Dim the night.

The immigrant's collections

A violent order is disorder; and a great disorder is an order. These two things are one.
    Wallace Stevens

A collector collects for the love of the thing.
Apparently he loves empty glass jars
and empty buckets of HTH pool chlorine
and rusted nuts and bolts and screws
and trowels and hammers and nail clippers
and blunt scissors and hose attachments
and nozzles and empty boxes of
chronic medication for hypertension.

*

The smoky murk of the workshop:
slabs of wood resting on steel drawers
brought home from the factory. Food cans
set on surfaces, up against the walls, beneath
shelves on brackets he had made, sprouting
brushes and sharp things, queuing like a row
of steampunk porcupines. The crazy
organised trays. Earless cups with cable ties.
Envelopes marked in his spikey script
with the names of seeds on them.
Slide boxes with tacks. Cutlery trays of screws.

*

The trick to borrowing something without asking
was to value each cog in this violent order equally.
Then you marked the place and returned
what you'd borrowed precisely. Before 6pm.

The Shasta daisy's native range

The wild Shasta daisy grows from seed like a classic perennial. But once established, it is permanent and never invasive.

Every early summer, Shasta daisies
whitewashed a strip of garden beyond
the kitchen window whose sill held little
bowls of drying seeds. Always little bowls
of seed and the white return of cheerful Shastas
around the same time the jasmine opened its legs
and warmed the courtyard with things I longed for.
My father, though, he loved those Shastas.
Because of his accent, I thought for years
that they were called Chester daisies.
Have you seen the Chester daisies?
Not wait for me to answer, and say
beautiful, drawing out the first
syllable and making a d of the t.
I would crane absently over the sill
and mmmm. Only now do I see
the southern sun in their yellow
bellybuttons, the fractals at their
centres, their simple hair-dos
nodding yesyesyes in the breeze.
How little they demanded of him,
how compliant they were. How
attractive their simple
perennial solace.

The garden

The willow tree the lemon tree the bottle brush
(front and side) the jasmine creeper the grape trellis
the herb corner the vegetable patch the compost heap
the fern outside my bedroom window the honeysuckle
on the wall of the neighbours' garage which abutted
our backyard the roses on the boundary morning shade
the Shasta daisies the strelitzia the monkey apple tree
the row of conifers by the pool and that bush that made
the tiniest creamy flowers which I used to think I would
want as confetti at my wedding if I ever got married.

Hybrids

What were you planting and uprooting,
autodidact of turf and drought and flame-torch sun?
You never planted your bones here. Perhaps
you planted the nerves at the centre of your bones.
You grew hybrid languages and hybrid children.
Unlike God, you were not pleased.

The existence of home

And you could never abjure your birthright
though you never went back. What for?
And you could never accept your permanence.

Everything chafed. But it was you all along: rubbing
your own sun-browned skin raw against the hemispheres,
always suspecting the existence of home.

Learning to swim

The hot lycra of my tube trainer smelt of the sea
when you opened your arms, and said jump! jump!
when I was only three. Along our edges, the pool flutter
of shouting and diving and screeching, but here
a halo of arms waiting in the water.

The blue of sky and pool washed over my head and through me
as I jumped and jumped. The laughter and water,
all the way through me, the splutter of us,
of me and you, me and you in the water.
I was the world's first and only daughter.

and now my mouth is small and hard
and now my tongue's a fossil
now my lips are bone on bone
my chest's an empty vessel.

Praxis – four steps to understanding change

i.   the wheels are coming off
(a found poem)

While a wheel bearing
must support its share
of the vehicle's weight,
it must also maintain
a perfect radial alignment
with the axle. The instant
it does not, the rotor
pushes the caliper pistons
into their bores and drags
against the pads. Noise

is a classic sign
of a bad wheel bearing:
snapping, clicking or popping.
Grinding, knocking or clunking.
Humming, rumbling or growling.

You may also feel it:

vibration or wobble,
shudder or shimmy,
abnormal side pull when
the brakes are applied.

In extreme cases,
internal and external
sensors can be
damaged from
excessive movement
caused by too much
endplay. This indicates
a lack or loss of
bearing clamp.

ii.   not co-opted

I give my mouth to no one.
I am the ears of everyone
and of my self. When you
shout, shells tilt. We nod.
We nod, the sea and I. We know.
We know. We lose ourselves in froth.

I will not staunch you.

I listen for a half beat,
a breath, and whisper back
the whispers of the waiting
gales. Pen-ink my voice
and silent so; willed to white,
whitened to bone. And flaccid.

iii. a shortish summary of revolution

nothing will remain
nothing will disappear
the old things will
make themselves
unmake themselves
the fire will burn nothing
will burn everything
everything is change
nothing is change
paint and flesh
and ink and hope
are fresh are old
will burn nothing will
remain everything will
stay the same.

iv.   ferocious

she loved her bedroom
made it her whole house
made it the private world

later when she was
an adult he would trail
his smelly fag in there
come in stand stare
half smiling
half waiting   (maybe)

for the forgiveness
that comes before an apology
or to marvel that she was grown
and was seldom afraid now.

Taped beak

seven songs of self-censorship

i.

seven songs
five and two
for the voiceless
listen now:

> seven
> songs
> seven
> strong
> times
> like
> doh
> ray
> me
> fa

oh there's nil
this song's
chords chime
me wrong
i'm tuning
all along
broken
staves

ii.

write what you know
i only know words
i know only nothing

iii.

over and over
christ this chorus bores me
i'm doing whatever the verb
is for litany and grass grows
over my feet   i am that woman
that white that wash that

i am my own thick black
censor lines my hushing
terrorist up-shutter

iv.

if there are no seeds in the pod
and no water in the bath
and no hope in the apple
if the notes are flat
and i clap ham-fisted
if i am mediocre
and count not a single
original thought
in the lines on my palm
and lack the courage of the sun
to rage on and on
why do i want to burn
paper under the whitewash of ink

v.

i dreamt my cover was blown
soon everyone would know
that i was young, gay, black -
and a man
my alter ego's twitter handle
was @hilaryvent

i taped her beak shut
now her eyes bulge

vi.

all i remember these days
is the tune of forgetting
the ghostly notation
between fading staves
where volume pitch and tone
have narrowed to the
ennui of a middle-c hum
but it's a start

vii.

the start
is the hardest part
and your breath
will catch you out
will catch you
your breath
could close you
your voice could
cloud into the
spaces between
your tongue and
the idea you had of
god

so don't start with god
that's the hardest part
begin with middle c
invoke god from

what's in-between

    (and what is it
    if it is not avarice
    to expect holiness
    from letters and notes
    and what is it
    if it is not greed
    to want more
    than one striving plea).

The things they do not tell you

Who else remembers the squeak and chafe of the gate,
the hoopoe in the bottlebrush or the way the grass
sank beneath the lightness of your small body's weight?

The hosepipe coiled on the path that lead to the front door,
fading slasto on the stoep, or the crack in the chimney
that grew wider every year as the house sank into the floor?

Unspeakable things were happening not far away
and they never told us. Never spoke of pity or complicity,
never said anything they could later downplay.

Does anyone remember that the brakes on the bike
churred and creaked? Does anyone remember the sound
of their own name in the mouth of their father, or the shrike,

or remember how in the morning each limb on the body awoke
in fear, hope, despair, wonder? Oh come. No one remembers
in abstracts. You like to think you recall the smell of smoke

but you were only eight and there were a hundred kilometres
between the dead child and the patterns you were tracing
on the kitchen linoleum that day long ago one winter.

Afer

i find that
with my hand flat
against the side
of your neck
under your ear
where your heart
echoes in slow pats
i can stop a great
wave of dust
where a continent
once lapped.

Weed

those who are footloose
who roam to the ends
of untethered threads
those with battered bags
and make-do those
whose assertions
to place are brief or twee
those who are home-free:

how were they released?

me, i am planted here, awake
and calcifying. my roots ache.

Rock fig

Tell them it's not just me who grows root-wild around the boulder
of this koppie. Exotic once and now endemic, we're all stubborn, but
unimportant. Ignore us. Long after they've cut us loose, we'll clench these
places in our root-fists.

i do not know
where i am now
you are stranger than milk
forgive me   the day begins and
doesn't end   it is a day without seam
and i do not know you here
                          i am unbuttoned
more naked than we've been most naked
nothing moves

Smoking

My aunt's speck of a planet
was a square house in a universe
of greying winter lawn. When we
pulled up in our Sunday
station wagon, she was standing
in the front garden wearing
red stovepipes. A cigarette
smoked itself in her right hand.

There must also have been Oros
and beans and sago pudding.
And chasing round the house with
cousins, and the allure of Archie
comics in a box under a bed.

But the best I can remember now
is that her Lexington pack matched
her trousers, and that it pleased me.

This is how dead people live on:
smiling in a shaft of memory
with smoke wreathing their heads.
A herald of hindsight.

Superstition

You're a machine, plugged in,
winched, pumping air into the
tubes and computers keeping
themselves alive via you. I've
lost count of the perforations
and plug points, the vents
and passages they've carved
into your skin. There is no place
for my hand or for anything not as thin
and cold as a needle. Only your
feet are uninvaded territory. They're
useless to these intricate calibrations.
But your feet are useful to me.
I can hold them and imagine
I'm steering you back here.

Do you remember the time when so many people we knew were dying?

You travel dark to the flat earth, but you pack light:
a few black items, some boundary stars. You will need nothing.

Above the ruler-line of the horizon, the clouds will do all that you cannot.
Look up: the cumulosaurus, the polar zeppelins, the thunderbears.

That is how to be big. You are stooped, not beneath clouds, but under
a coincidence of days of brittleness, pine coffins, rock-hard clocks,
and the twin shadows everywhere:
the simplicity of horizon, the rococo of clouds.

I write in these shadows. We drive out of the countryside,
past the Lazy Daisy Lodge and the catwalk between the koppies.
We milk the air. We travel home. Your beard is longer.
So much to do. So much. My patience bares its teeth.

Cleaning the wound

the trick is to pull off the plaster
and look the wound in the eye

it's not as bad as you think it will be
it's just a doorway

a threshold to sweep
and polish and protect.

Have you ever seen a maggot move?

You'd think they'd be sluggish.
But maggots gnaw fast
against their wingless childhood.
What's their hurry? They're
almost frantic against the press
of time, as though death is a thing
you hunt and trap if you move
with covert urgency. Rats too.

The sweet rot smell of rat
and maggot, their furtive speed,
pervert my dreams for weeks.

I shudder. I too move
with vermin haste.

First flush

You bake in your sleep.

You throw off the fleece.
You throw off the blanket.
You pull off your t-shirt.
You pull off your panties.
Your socks you rub off against the sheets.

Still, this heat rides you.

You put a leg out into the cold night.
An arm. Then you throw off the duvet –

you dive with lunatic limbs
into the frigid mid-winter night,
a dam that the high-hot summer mountain
holds in the burning cup of its hands.

January swim

The great advantage of being alive
                                   ee cummings

The mountains are still cooling.
The night was not long enough.
The morning bends over us. From
this rock I can slip almost soundlessly
into the amber. I own this body as though
I am its first citizen. To the middle then,
to command this day from the dam's belly.
I turn my face up to the lavender-hello and drift,
hairbeams streaming. Look, Sun.
An undone knot. A drifting speck.

Spring outing

our day in the daisies died early
while we spoke past one another
the coffee turned cold from indecision
i had wanted to walk alone the two of us
not to wash up on a stinking hazy shore
with fat men and their families camping
around their fat cars with cadacs and gazebos
and whining children arranged all around
and the mothers with their hopeful picnics
and the grandmothers with their useless hands
and the fathers the sitting drinking smoking fathers
with their two chins and their sausage fingers
and their four-by-four nonchalance.

What wedding is this?

This morning the mist-veiled
autumn mountain is all ours.

Leucadendrons' pink muzzles
line the path like dewy bridesmaids
wearing sparkles. An orb-web spider
reigns from the middle of her wagon wheel
turned chandelier by drops of dew
and tufts of light.

> *What wedding is this?*

In the dark bush, above the mist-slicked
rocks of the dry riverbed, moss grows
in the armpits of trees. Seed confettis the ground.
Older promises sweat from the stream's verterbra,
and the mountain's crotch smells like buchu and rooibos.

Oh, honeybush, this is not a wedding.
It's an ecstasy.

How the architect lives

At night alone in a tower
he draws the boxes
that will become rooms.
He shoots a digital diagonal
into space previously occupied
only by itself. He tilts a world
towards the sun to move the light,
and breaks horizons into heartbeats.
He unfurls fire escapes and draws lifts
up imaginary shafts. He raises roofs beyond
the call of geometry. He whispers at unbuilt corners
to coax a pulse into the veins hidden inside walls.
        Late. Late. Outside the window now
is a crashed constellation. He opens his palm
and blows on it till a small city pops up. He
doesn't think of clocks while he measures
the make-believe bathrooms and kitchens,
imagined here in this calculus of planning.
        Soon it will be done. Until then, he
works parallel to the ancient light,
dreaming it undreamt.

Rain

when the go-away bird
whooped and flopped from the bottlebrush,

and, on the strip of lawn
between the vibacrete wall
and the bedroom windows,
the roses' frilly throats smelt mauve,

the whole day could be pressed ripe
between clouds that stacked themselves
in blood and bruises
and the chlorine sparks left by lightning.

when chance and cloud agreed,
hot rain tapped bacteria spores
to loam the air i'd already bristled with
adolescence and impatience.

last night, when we kissed
i felt sunken in that highveld
late afternoon. a garden grew up.
your mouth smelt of rain.

Truffler

I, the earth and hot,
swell my fruiting bodies
for the hog's horny snuffling.
In root arms that wade
beneath bush and compost
I hide salty treats,
and resist, but only just,
his snouting.
He noses folds,
balls clods aside with his face -
a trotter ready, but unequal.
He plays the mild hunter,
nudging and ruffling
underbrush and mud,
and I, oh,
loose-limbed and louche and lucky,
until sods are so loosed
I thrum the lumps and pillows
of my ground bed. He finds the
summer truffle, tosses it up
and mouths it from the sky,
where a slow melting
morning toffees over.

Bright star

the years pile up i don't know how
against the un-ageing mountain
in spite of corrosive winds
under the sun's dragging fingers

back when you were still a little cruel
we went to the six o'clock show
of the movie about the poor poet
and his bright star and i wept and wept

you squeezed my hand and didn't know
but maybe you did that i wept for everything
and all of it: the sun, the wind, and our
infinitesimal belligerent important
      little love.

Shunt

The train that shook the house
punched such fear into my fast heart
that I stared with blind eyes
at the curtains stirring too soft in the half-moon light,
my back rigid against your hushing hands.

Nothing
          then made sense.
 I could bridle

nothing
          with the train's trail so close
the bed rattled our feet.
And I could brace

nothing
          against your equivocations.

          Unruly love.
          Death's only antonym.

I shudder alive against the track,
wait for one thousand devil carriages to pass
before I bear me back.

i knew no goodness till i'd trawled
the sky of his forehead for the bitter stars
and found none.

Pathfinders

The native guide to lead you through the blankness of this map is you.
        Nick Laird

i.

Hairy larva.
Furry curl.
Caterpillars this fat
could squelch
in the echo chamber
of memory forever.
She nicked
her wheel on time,
and whooped
the near miss -
her triumph just a
death-delaying wish.

ii.

It's possible to paddle up a tune,
whipping wind into the spokes
as though pumping an accordion
or bagpipes, but without the notes.
So she wheezed music from rubber
on asphalt and grit, a rushing frrr,
the sound of vacuum and of space,
the sound of sleep unconscious
of itself, of thought on a silent face.

Then there was a gate, a slowing,
a stopping, a dismounting. A chock-sound
as the gate fell back against its frame.

Back in the saddle, the web,
unstuck from its waiting, snatched
at cheeks and brows and lashes,
so she blew and picked and spat,
but chugged the pedals that flashed
and winked at gulls and terns.

Pump. Grind. Blow. Cruise.

Fuck the creatures who tried lay claim;
there were quavers she wouldn't lose.

iii.

The island roses, recently livid
had paled and stretched,
lolling along the lane, whoring
their scent at gravid horizons.

iv.

Rain drummed an
earthworm
on to the path.
It writhed madly.

Skinned pink.
A raw knot.

She hated it hotly.

v.

The small white butterfly she swallowed
on the bike track made her teeth tingle.

In her throat it paused to close
then open its wings.
A pitch perfect *la* leapt
at the breeze and was swept
back like a paper scrap.

> (Further in, it settled on her sternum
> widened its span but, finding itself small
> against the great Lepidoptera of lungs,
>
> flitted to her stomach, where
> it was too alone for anxiety.)

By the time she'd peddled
to the end of the track,
her backpack had rigged white sails.

She snicked a turn and scudded home
where she bent to reap
a small white *la* from the mat.

Then why

look, she said,
it's binary code:
black and white,
all made and
remade from the
vaults of nought
& the arrows of one.

her eyes were stripes
against the sun, her
mouth an o.

we make,
that's all, the pen
the brush the drill
the wood the tool
the trowel, your hand -

stippling the edges of nought
containing a filigree
of night-framed thought
swaying the lines
scratching the edge
toothing some surface
holding the strain
straining the end
curving what's plain.

i said: my head is sore.
she said: halo-ache, ah!
hail the burr the coronet
the fuzzy crown
the blister the weal.

it hurts, i said.
here, she said,
pouring ink
into my palm.

it's medicine.

Native

I dream in
the universal tongue
of metaphor
in arcane horror
in hot pulsing
in mammal guts.
I dream in
the borderless interior
where migraines fizz
towards the light
and galleons are
let loose to gulp
at meager winds.
I dream in
tongues more ancient
than the baby's skull
where scarring tissue
burns trails of smoke
where eyes water
in the bright murk
where my children
grown giant
escape danger
I can't protect
them from.
I dream in
the alphabet of dance
where consonants
have fur
where vowels bleat
where vague
and precise
are the same
impossible

achievement.
I dream triple-tongued
the insides of my
cheeks scaled
my throat a gill
a slit of membrane
across an all-seeing eye.
I dream
omnivorous.
I dream
in vex
in shift
in slant.
I speak transparent.

When I finally get to Bhutan

I will have to eat stars to be guided back.
The Southern Cross on my wrist. I will have to hold
Orion's belt out to him. I will have to know
that the dust I breathe is home dirt just so
that I can carry it all back, carry it all on my back.
I will stand at the bare feet of Gangkhar Puensum
with Venus in my armpit and wind-dogs
at my ankles. I will wait there for a passport
or a transit bus or a bridge or loose roots
and think about the last climb. I will not climb.
I will drink a cup of water while I wait. I will be glad
to go home.

The first time we went for a walk

We walked all the way to the beach
along the sand into some sort of
cosmological crack where we met
back then before the beginning
and the ends of things and collected milk,
plucked it, fruit-finds, held in the webs
between our fingers, and older things
and things untold and younger,
and then back again to a wooden deck
where a wind rustled and you dusted
sea sand from between my toes.
My feet were at home in your lap.

Notes and acknowledgements

I would like to thank Indra Wussow of the Sylt Foundation for the month-long residency on the island of Sylt, during which time some of these poems, particularly the "Pathfinders" cycle, came into being.

The last line of "The existence of home" is my translation from a line in *Huilboek* by Ryk Hattingh ("Om vir altyd die bestaan van 'n tuiste te vermoed.")

The found poem "The wheels are coming off" is from knowyourparts.com

"Afer" is a Latin word meaning "of or pertaining to Africa".

Some of the poems in this collection were first published elsewhere:

"How the architect lives" and "January swim" (*New Contrast* Manifesto Edition, Vol. 44, 2016)
"Shunt" (*Paris Lit Up*, 2013)
"Pathfinders" (*The Sol Plaatje European Union Poetry Anthology*, Vol. III, 2013)
"Then why" was written for inclusion in the Burr Print & Purpose print portfolio curated by Eunice Geustyn and Melvyn Minnaar for AVA in 2016.

Printed in the United States
By Bookmasters